Working in College Sports

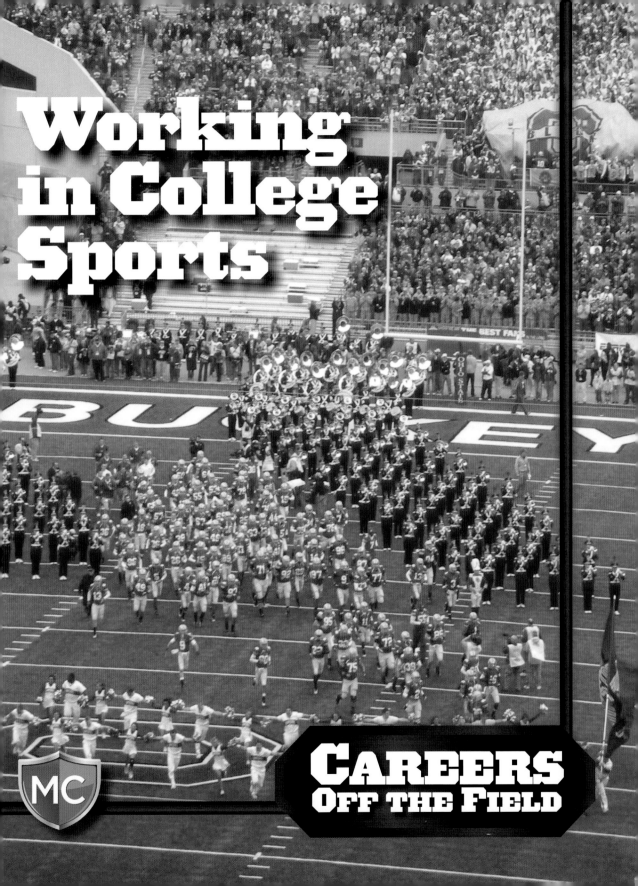

CAREERS OFF THE FIELD

CAREERS
OFF THE FIELD

Working in College Sports

By Michael Burgan

Mason Crest
450 Parkway Drive, Suite D
Broomall, PA 19008
www.masoncrest.com

Printed and bound in the United States of America.

Series ISBN: 978-1-4222-3264-4
Hardback ISBN: 978-1-4222-3274-3
EBook ISBN: 978-1-4222-8532-9

First printing
1 3 5 7 9 8 6 4 2

Produced by Shoreline Publishing Group LLC
Santa Barbara, California
Editorial Director: James Buckley Jr.
Designer: Bill Madrid
Production: Sandy Gordon
www.shorelinepublishing.com

Cover photo: Aceshot1/Shutterstock

Library of Congress Cataloging-in-Publication Data is on file with the publisher

CONTENTS

Key Icons to Look For

Words to Understand: These words with their easy-to-understand definitions will increase the reader's understanding of the text, while building vocabulary skills.

Sidebars: This boxed material within the main text allows readers to build knowledge, gain insights, explore possibilities, and broaden their perspectives by weaving together additional information to provide realistic and holistic perspectives.

Research Projects: Readers are pointed toward areas of further inquiry connected to each chapter. Suggestions are provided for projects that encourage deeper research and analysis.

Text-Dependent Questions: These questions send the reader back to the text for more careful attention to the evidence presented here.

Series Glossary of Key Terms: This back-of-the-book glossary contains terminology used throughout this series. Words found here increase the reader's ability to read and comprehend higher-level books and articles in this field.

Foreword

By Al Ferrer

So you want to work in sports? Good luck! You've taken a great first step by picking up this volume of CAREERS OFF THE FIELD. I've been around sports professionally—on and off the field, in the front office, and in the classroom—for more than 35 years. My students have gone on to work in all the major sports leagues and for university athletic programs. They've become agents, writers, coaches, and broadcasters. They were just where you are now, and the lessons they learned can help you succeed.

One of the most important things to remember when looking for a job in sports is that being a sports fan is not enough. If you get an interview with a team, and your first sentence is "I'm your biggest fan," that's a kiss of death. They don't want fans, they want pros. Show your experience, show who you know, show how you can contribute.

Another big no-no is to say, "I'll do anything." That makes you a non-professional or a wanna-be. You have to do the research and find out what area is best for your personality and your skills. This book series will be a vital tool for you to do that research, to find out what areas in sports are out there, what kind of people work in them, and where you would best fit in.

And that leads to my third point: Know yourself. Look carefully at your interests and skills. You need to understand what you're good at and how you like to work. If you get energy from being around people, then you don't want to be in a room with a computer because you'll go nuts. You want to be in the action around people, so you might look at sales or marketing or media relations or being an agent. But if you're more comfortable being by yourself, then you look at analysis, research, perhaps the numbers side of scouting or recruiting. So you have to know yourself.

And you have to manage your expectations. There is a lot of money in sports but unless you are a star athlete, you probably won't be making much in your early years.

I'm not trying to be negative, but I want to be realistic. I've loved every minute of my life in sports. If you have a passion for sports and you can bring professionalism and quality work—and you understand your expectations—you can have a great career. But just like the athletes we admire, you have to prepare, you have to work hard, and you have to never, ever quit.

Series consultant Al Ferrer founded the sports management program at the University of California, Santa Barbara, after an award-winning career as a Division I baseball coach. Along with his work as a professor, Ferrer is an advisor to pro and college teams, athletes, and sports businesses.

Introduction

Words To Understand

alumni: people who graduate from a particular college

intercollegiate: something that takes places between two schools, such as a sporting event

junior colleges: schools that offer two years of courses as opposed to four

recruiting: the process of finding the best athletes to play for a team

revenue: money earned from a business or event

Game Day

At colleges and universities across the United States, Saturday afternoon in the fall means one thing: football. In college athletics, football draws the biggest crowds and provides many schools with needed revenue. Many games are televised, helping the colleges and universities spread their names beyond their home cities and states. And for alumni, those football games give them a chance to go back to their school, meet old friends, and feel proud when their team wins.

At larger schools, football is big business, and at the best of those programs, such as the University of Alabama, the successful football program helps pay for other **intercollegiate** sports. On the field, the game is about athletic skill. But around and outside the football stadium, dozens and perhaps even hundreds of people have worked to make that game happen.

At smaller schools and **junior colleges**, sports might not bring in as much money as big-time football, but they attract student athletes looking to compete after high school. The sports programs also serve as a rallying point for other students, alumni, and local communities. At most schools, students take part in recreational sports for fun and exercise, too.

The popularity of college athletics creates many job opportunities for people who love sports but aren't college athletes themselves. In many cases, the skills people need for these college athletic jobs are the same ones they would use in parallel careers in the business world. Making money, marketing a "product," and creating a positive image are essential in both worlds.

As people who work in college athletics stress, however, their field has a major difference. They get to see young men and women develop both as athletes and students and to bond with them.

"You don't get that in another industry," said Mark Massari, deputy athletic director at Oregon State University. For Massari and others, building that connection and seeing the student-athletes mature, "is what [the job] is all about."

The Business of College Sports

These numbers from *USA Today* show how much money is at stake in college athletics. They show the revenues that sports generated for ten leading Division I schools in 2013.

Texas	$165,691,486
Wisconsin	$149,141,405
Alabama	$143,776,550
Michigan	$143,514,125
Ohio State	$139,639,307
Florida	$130,011,244
Oklahoma	$123,805,661
LSU	$117,457,398
Oregon	$115,241,070
Tennessee	$111,579,779

Getting to Game Day

Athletic directors (ADs) at all levels and the people who work with them make college sports happen. Looking at the complete variety of jobs available off the field is beyond the scope of this book. Instead, it will focus on ADs like Mark Massari, who oversee a broad range of people: communications experts who work in sports information departments; facilities people who prepare stadiums and courts whenever athletes need them; and people who handle the business side of college sports. That includes making sure everyone gets paid and follows all the rules of college athletics.

Before the kickoff of that typical Saturday football game, fundraisers in the athletic department might have sought money to help pay for a new indoor training room. Individual donors might give several million dollars to help build new facilities, and the school staff wants to make sure they feel valued. Fundraising also means seeking much smaller donations by sending out letters and making calls to thousands of people.

Members of the AD's staff also seek money from corporations, as they buy ads in the arenas or sponsor contests during breaks in the game. The companies promote their goods and services while associating with an institution with devoted fans.

In another part of the athletics department, members of the communications department gathered information on their school's players to share with the reporters and broadcasters covering the game. Kyle Muncy, former sports information director (SID) at the University of Connecticut (UConn), said that when sports fans hear TV broadcasters reciting details about a player, "It is the SID staff pulling that information together and providing it to the TV people."

Even before the season started, people behind the scenes were working toward getting that fall football game underway. **Recruiting** the best athletes is a major part of a coach's job in any sport, but athletic directors play a role, too. They meet with top-level recruits and their parents to make sure the school and student are a good fit for each other. The ADs also hire—and sometimes fire—the coaches, seeking men and women who can bring victory on the playing field while assuring the athletes' success in the classroom.

Students interested in health careers can keep a hand in sports by working as athletic trainers for schools.

Closer to the field, college workers on game day put down fresh lines to mark the yards and the end zones. That follows months of preparation by the school's grounds crew to ensure both grass and turf fields are in top condition. Other workers make sure each team has all the equipment it needs on the sidelines. And sports medicine experts are standing by, ready to treat injured athletes.

A career in college athletics off the field can be exciting and rewarding. It can also be demanding. But it's a good fit for people who love sports and a college environment.

Words To Understand

academic: relating to classes and studies

conferences: groups of schools in which schools within a group play each other frequently in sports

internships: positions that rarely offer pay but provide on-the-job experience

undergraduate: a person pursuing a four-year college degree or something related to such a program

minors: programs that let students concentrate on a specific area of study but without receiving a degree

Getting Started

When soccer player Kyle Muncy transferred to the University of Connecticut, it was not the best academic move. He was interested in studying communications, but then, in the mid-1980s, the program at UConn was geared more toward the science of communication—the structure of languages, for example. Muncy was more interested in broadcast communications, especially in sports.

Under the rules of the National Collegiate Athletics Administration (NCAA), as a transfer Muncy had to sit out a year before he could play on Connecticut's soccer team. That year off, though, gave him his big break in sports communications. He had the chance to broadcast the soccer games over the school's radio station. In that job, he got to know people in the communications department. One important conversation came during his senior year, when he talked to one department member after an away game. "I said, would you mind if we sat together on the ride home," Muncy recalled. "I'd love to talk to you about what you do and if there's any opportunities to get involved as a student."

That staff member arranged for an **internship** the following year, which led to Muncy's getting a full-time job in the department—the first steps in his eventually becoming UConn's SID.

The NCAA and College Divisions

The National Collegiate Athletic Association is made up of more than 1,200 schools, conferences, and other organizations tied to college sports. The NCAA tries to make sure that student athletes balance their studies and their sports in a way that benefits them and allows fair competition between schools. The colleges and universities range in size from just a few hundred students to 40,000 or more. A school's size and its ability to fund a certain number of sports for both men and women determines in which of the NCAA's three divisions it plays. Division I includes the largest, most famous sports schools, such as the University of Alabama, Notre Dame, and Stanford. Divisions II and III have smaller public and private colleges. Some small schools join another organization—the National Association of Intercollegiate Athletics (NAIA). In general, the largest schools in Division I offer the most job opportunities in athletics and recreational sports, though every school that has athletic teams needs people off the field to run their sports programs.

Muncy had a good academic background for his position, thanks to his communications degree. But he also took the steps many veterans of college athletics say are key to landing a job in the field. Talk to people at your school who do what you would like to do. Volunteer. Seek internships. And be ready to do anything to gain knowledge and meet people who can help you later on.

Choosing a College and a Major

For some careers, such as medicine, students need to follow an academic track to get a job. They might also spend several years working under the supervision of people licensed in their field. Landing a job in college athletics is a little different. Oregon State's Mark Massari studied history while an **undergraduate**. William Husak, athletic director at Loyola Marymount University (LMU) in Los Angeles, studied and then taught physical education for years before taking over at LMU. While that academic background was related to sports, it did not include the kind of skills he needed to become an AD.

In the past, Husak said, "The old football coach became the athletic director when he could no longer coach football."

Today, colleges and universities expect different skills from an AD, depending on their particular needs. Some ADs might have a law degree or a master's degrees in business. Some might have worked for professional sports teams. What they share is a love of college athletics and the ability to meet the needs of their particular school.

First in the Nation

Before 1966, someone looking to study sports management in college was out of luck. But that year, Ohio University introduced the first academic program to focus on that field, when it offered a master's in sports administration. Today the university's School of Sports Administration offers both bachelor's and master's programs. For undergraduates, the school stresses getting practical experience through internships and jobs. Graduate students can pursue a degree online, though they still have to spend some time on campus. (Other schools offer online graduate degrees as well). Ohio University prides itself on finding jobs for its students, thanks to the contacts of its professors and alumni.

Sports Management

In the past, getting a degree in physical education might have led to a career in college sports. Today, the preferred program for many jobs is called sports management. Over the past 35 years, the number of schools that offer sports management courses has exploded, with more than 300 offering at least a bachelor's degree. Top schools offering the degree include the University of

Massachusetts at Amherst, Ohio University, and the University of Central Florida. Schools also offer **minors** in sports management for students who want to focus on another academic area while still gaining knowledge about sports administration.

The increase in these programs reflects the enthusiasm people have for working in college athletics. Competition is tough in intercollegiate sports, but recreational sports programs are expanding at many colleges, reflecting the desire of students to engage in athletics even if they aren't competing against other schools. Those growing rec programs also translate into more job opportunities.

In a typical sports management program, students study such things as the ethics of sports, how to run facilities, the laws and finances related to sports, sports marketing, and how to manage

Helping run gyms used by all students can be part of working in college sports.

other people. Along with the courses that focus on sports, the students also take general business courses. Computer skills are always a plus, and a background in graphic design is useful for students interested in some kind of communications job.

High school students interested in pursuing sports management in college should consider several factors. Husak recommended that they seek a university that offers the kind of environment that they would eventually like to work in. "If you want to be at a football school, get involved in some way… with a football program. If you want to be involved at Division II, get yourself into a Division II area." While it's preferable that the student's initial involvement be in athletics, it's not mandatory. Bright students with a passion for sports are sometimes able to find jobs in an athletic department.

People with an interest in physical therapy and training can find work in a college gym or with a college athletic department.

Other things to think about when choosing a college include the emphasis on the sports management program and where the school is located. Some schools house the program in the department of kinesiology—the study of movement, especially as it relates to sports. Other schools put their sports management programs in their business school. In a kinesiology program, students might not be required to take courses related to business, such as marketing and accounting. They would have to take them on their own, since a knowledge of business is crucial for many jobs in athletics.

For students who don't want to pursue a sports marketing degree, other useful degree programs include:

- Communications or marketing, for someone interested in media relations, marketing, or public relations
- Health-related degrees, to become an athletic trainer or physical therapist
- Business, finance, or accounting, to get involved in the financial side of college athletics
- Exercise and sports science, which stresses physical education and can lead to such jobs as a strength and fitness coach or another athletics-related position

Paul Swangard, of the Warsaw Sports Marketing Center at the University of Oregon, thinks having a degree that doesn't focus on sports can be helpful down the road. He told *Bloomberg Businessweek* that some students pursue sports management degrees "and ten years later they don't want to do sports anymore—that degree won't be as flexible."

It Really Is Who You Know

A school's location can influence what kind of sports internships are available. In cities with a number of pro teams or athletic organizations, such as New York, Los Angeles, or Indianapolis, internships might be easier to come by. At some schools, interns earn college credit for this work. Competition for these positions is tough, but the experts agree that internships are a valuable part of the education process.

Carolyne Savini works for Turnkey Sports and Entertainment, which fills open jobs with sports teams and college athletic departments. She told *Forbes*, "For anyone trying to break into the sports industry at the entry level, internship experience is critical. Short of an inside connection, I rarely, if ever, see someone get hired into a job without previous internship experience."

Working as an intern either during or after college provides another key part of finding a job: networking. Meeting people, asking them about their jobs, and having them introduce you to others in the field are key to making the connections that lead to jobs.

Tyler Geivett, assistant athletic director of communications at Loyola Marymount University, said getting an internship in media relations when he was a student at that school was key for setting him on his career path. Whether as an intern or student, Geivett stressed the importance of networking.

"Don't be afraid to introduce yourself to people," Geivett said. "You might be working alongside another intern, but then they get a big break." Keeping in touch with coworkers makes it easier to get a helping hand from those people if they do get that break.

Another way to make those connections is to volunteer in the athletics department, especially in a student's main area of interest. "Today, the foot in the door is sometimes volunteering," said William Husak. The key is "doing something that makes them unable to see life without you." Impressing those in charge might lead them to create a spot for the volunteer, or make him or her the first choice when a job is vacant.

Advanced Degrees

Having some sort of graduate degree is increasingly common in college athletics. A growing number of schools offer a master's in sports management. Many more offer master's in sports medicine. Some people pursue a master's of business administration, and some schools include sports management courses within that program. At the next level, some schools also offer a Ph.D. or doctor of education (Ed.D.) in sports management.

To aim for just about any key job in an athletic department, excelling in the classroom is the first step.

Outside of sports medicine, there are no set career paths for jobs in college athletics. Athletic directors, though, can benefit by earning a Ph.D., as it often sets them apart from other candidates for top jobs. And schools that stress academics might prefer an AD who has that degree and experience as a professor.

While educational background is important, most people in college athletics stress the personality traits that help recent graduates find jobs and advance. They take the initiative and look for things to do, rather than waiting to be asked. Jon Spaventa is the director of the recreation department at the University of California, Santa Barbara. He has spent several decades in college athletics and said the people who succeed "show up early for work and stay late" and are "constantly looking for ways to grow and do more."

Text-Dependent Questions

1. What did most people in this chapter say was the key first step in finding a job in college sports?

2. What are some advanced degrees that might help a person get a job as an athletic director?

3. Name some interpersonal skills that are useful in college sports.

Research Project

Find out which colleges in your state or close by offer a sports management degree of some kind. What kind of classes do they offer?

Words To Understand

compliance: the action of following rules

postseason: games played after a team's regular season ends, such as in a conference tournament

renovating: improving or updating an existing building

Hard at Work

A college athletic department is like its own company, and the products it's selling are the school's various teams. It's no wonder that sports management degrees and business courses—if not actual work experience in business—are increasingly helpful for people seeking jobs in college athletics.

That athletics-as-business model is most apparent at the larger Division I schools that emphasize football. Pat Haden (at left) became USC's athletic director after a career in the legal profession (though he was also a college and NFL player). It's one reason why more schools are hiring ADs with a background in business, not intercollegiate sports administration. And the athletics department is just one part of an even larger business—the university itself. For many of the people under the AD, they must realize their role in building the business and protecting the brand—the good name of the school and its sports teams.

The Internal and the External

Many college athletic departments are split into internal and external areas, just as many businesses are. Internal departments include the business office, which tries to make sure revenues and expenses are in balance and that everyone gets paid, and facilities grounds staff. Another internal area is academic advising or counseling; sports teams want to make sure their student athletes do well in school. Partly this is to help the students get the best education possible, but the NCAA penalizes schools that don't meet certain academic requirements for student athletes who receive scholarships. Penalties include reducing the number of scholarships a school can give or not being allowed to compete in **postseason** play.

To make sure they follow NCAA rules on academics, recruiting, and other issues, most schools have **compliance** offices. A legal background can be helpful for this kind of work. A compliance office makes sure the athletic department also follows the school's own rules, and, at times, state and federal laws as well. William Husak of Loyola Marymount said the concern over being compliant with the many rules is not limited to the compliance office. "Everybody's job has some portion of it dealing with compliance."

People with a flair for numbers and analysis tend to do well on the internal side, particularly in the business office. For the external side, an ability to communicate well and get along with people is key. The external includes such departments as communications, marketing, ticket sales, and fundraising. For Mark Massari at Oregon State, the realization of the importance of fundraising came when he was a college athlete. "Somebody donated for me to have a scholarship," he said, and with that awareness, and given his own personality, he thought fundraising for a college was something he could do after he graduated.

Coping With Compliance

Compliance with rules and regulations, especially those set down by the NCAA, is a major concern in college athletics. The NCAA rules manual runs hundreds of pages, and schools are expected to watch for and report rules violations on their own. In recent years, some schools have hired compliance officers who previously worked for the NCAA enforcing the rules. One of those was Angie Cretors. She had been with the NCAA for ten years before going to work for the University of Connecticut in 2013. Her old job, she told *Sports Business Daily*, had burnt her out. "You always kind of see the negatives when you're in enforcement. You're dealing with people that are possibly or alleged to have violated the rules, so you're kind of always viewed as the enemy." She welcomed the chance to help the school catch violations before they became major problems. Connecticut had earlier been penalized for breaking NCAA rules, forcing its men's basketball team to miss the postseason in 2013.

Schools often look to hire people with fundraising skills they acquired outside of sports. The financial pressure is high for public colleges, which rely on state funding and face budget cuts during tough economic times, such as the country experienced in the early 2000s. Small private schools that don't have the wealthy alumni larger schools do also have that pressure.

On the Job

Given the wide range of jobs in college athletics, people might find themselves sitting in an office every day, traveling to meet recruits or fundraisers, or spending some time in an office while also attending games throughout a season. The job requirements can also vary by the sport. For Tyler Geivett of Loyola Marymount, preparing information for the media is a large part of his job. He has to provide statistics on his teams, help set up interviews, and at times coordinate information with the opposing school's sports information department. But a major sport, such as basketball, will draw more reporters than a swim meet, so he has more work to do before and after basketball games.

Geivett and other communications staffers also keep tabs on social media. Schools now often have digital or social media coordinators who promote the schools' teams and individual athletes on such digital platforms as Facebook and Twitter. Those jobs didn't exist ten years ago, and future changes in technology could create new positions.

Social media, Geivett said, "has certainly allowed smaller schools to get more coverage than they once did." A tweet about a particular athlete, for example, might be picked up by much larger media outlets and then spread among their users. Sports information departments also monitor what athletes post, to

LMU's Geivett is a jack-of-all-trades. Here, he takes over as the announcer at a baseball game.

make sure they don't accidentally break an NCAA rule, such as promoting a certain kind of shoe or energy drink.

As in the communication department, game day is a busy time for people in charge of a school's athletic facilities. For Jon Spaventa and his staff, it means making sure lines are painted on fields and lights work in gyms or for outdoor night games. Spaventa's staff includes event specialists, who are at the

Some jobs in an athletic department are responsible for managing the upkeep of athletic fields.

games and meets to make sure everything goes smoothly, and coordinators who hire and train students to work the events.

Overseeing all the activity is the top person in a school's athletic department, the athletic director. ADs have many responsibilities, but the best of them know how to choose the right assistants and let them handle many of those responsibilities. For William Husak, the key is to "stay out of the details…and paint broad brush visions of what's possible," and then work with others to create the plan that achieves that vision.

On a typical day Husak might meet with a donor off campus, have meetings back at school with staff and coaches, and also talk to the school's administrators. Husak also watches as many games as he can. Under him and most athletic directors are a number of associate or assistant athletic directors assigned to supervise a particular area, such as business, media, and compliance.

Benefits of the Job

Talk to anyone in college athletics, and the same message comes up again and again. Almost any position requires someone who is willing to work hard. Kyle Muncy is wary of students looking for a job who "may just want to get a seat at the basketball game or

Keeping Athletes Healthy

When players are injured on the field, they know that trained professionals are nearby to treat the injury and help with their recovery. Sports medicine is a growing field at all levels, and college teams rely on athletic trainers as the first person on the scene when an injury happens. The trainers work with team doctors and medical specialists, such as surgeons and physical therapists (PTs), to help the athletes return to peak performance. In some cases, PTs also work with athletes to prevent injuries before they occur. That can involve giving the athletes exercises or examining their body movements to make sure they are not putting stress on their muscles and joints. People interested in sports medicine pursue specialized degrees and most have at least a master's degree. While getting their graduate degree, students can often work as assistants in their school's athletic training department. Athletic trainers are employees of their school, but team doctors and physical therapists usually have their own practice.

at the football game." When the season ends for one sport, another is starting, and assistant ADs or people in communications often handle multiple sports. But with the hard work come rewards that go beyond a paycheck and the chance to be involved with sports.

For people like athletic trainers and communication staff, who spend a lot of time with the athletes both home and away, their job lets them connect with the students on a personal level. "You get to know them," said Tyler Geivett, "they start to trust you. And you're getting to know a person who potentially could be a future superstar."

A long bus ride might give some people in athletics

a quiet moment alone with student athletes. But there are also the high-energy moments, such as after a big win. "The minute after the horn sounds at the end," said Kyle Muncy, reflecting on his days as UConn's SID,

When the team wins, you win. Department workers celebrate in different ways than players, however.

"and I would be out on the court, grabbing Coach [Jim] Calhoun for an interview...I knew there were people who were looking and saying, 'Man, that guy has the best job ever.'"

From the top spot, AD William Husak gets a number of pleasures from his job. It's rewarding when he can add a new sports program, or when he sees student-athletes get their degree in four years. Being around those young people, he said, "helps to keep you young and vibrant and energetic." He also thinks that athletic departments attract "positive, can-do people," which creates a positive work environment. For ADs and others in athletic departments, having winning programs also creates a lot of positive energy.

Sometimes the rewards of college athletics come from teamwork not connected to a sport. At the University of California, Santa Barbara (UCSB), students can vote on whether they want to spend money, perhaps as much as $15 million, for designated projects such as **renovating** a gym. Jon Spaventa

Raising money to keep athletic facilities up-to-date—or finding funds to build new stadiums—is a big part of many athletic departments.

has worked several times with student leaders who collected signatures to put sports facility renovations on a ballot and found support to get the money approved. He said, "When…you've worked together and been successful and you know you're going to have these great facilities because of it, those are wonderful experiences."

No matter what they do, the staff of college athletic departments find satisfaction in their jobs, no matter if their teams win or lose.

Text-Dependent Questions

1. What are the two parts that most athletic departments are made of?

2. When athletic directors hire people to assist them, what are some of the qualities you think they look for?

3. What are some of the key jobs of the events staff before an athletic contest?

Research Project

Let's say you want to be an athletic trainer. Go online and look for the requirements to be licensed in your state. What is the educational background needed and what kind of exams must one pass? See if you can find out what the average pay for that job is in your state or your area.

Words To Understand

benefits: insurance, vacation time, or extra things an employee receives in addition to a salary

burnout: stress or demands from a job that make workers feel drained and less interested in their work

compliant: successfully following the rules of an organization

sunshine laws: laws that make some government information, such as what employees get paid or messages they send, public information

Realities of the Workplace

Working for a school's sports team can seem glamorous, with many events attracting large crowds and national TV coverage. But each job in college athletics also has its own challenges. And even getting that job can be tough.

Competition is stiff for certain positions. People who aspire to work their way up to an AD job at a major school face this reality: there are only about 350 Division I positions available. Even adding in schools in the other two divisions and junior colleges, in 2014 the United States had about 7,000 institutions offering two- and four-year undergraduate degrees. Not all of them have sports programs, and on average only several hundred new schools open each year. Those numbers show that getting that top spot in college athletics is not easy.

Competition can be hard for other jobs, too. Even the

largest Division I schools may only have five to ten positions in such departments as the business office, compliance, and communications. Students seeking careers in college athletics might have to start at smaller schools and be open to moving

Organizing and managing rec sports on campus can be a great way to get started in sports management.

to any geographic area. With experience, they may be able to land a job at a larger school, but there are no guarantees.

Recreational sports on college campuses might be one place with more jobs becoming available. Jon Spaventa noted the growing popularity of sports clubs on many campuses, which creates support positions. At his school, he said, "We're doing the same kinds of things in recreational sports that are being done in intercollegiate athletics, which is . . . doubling the job opportunities."

What the Job Pays

Al Ferrer has been a college baseball coach and a professor of sports management. When it comes to pay, he said that people in athletics can expect their salaries to start out as "dirt, then it's going to be human, and then it's winning the lottery...it's a pyramid, getting to that lottery." Ferrer added that people who find their salary rising slowly or get married and start families might find it's time to take their skills to the business world, where salaries for comparable positions are usually higher.

In college athletics in particular, even the top of the pyramid might not result in a huge salary for all but top-

Women in College Athletics

For women seeking jobs in athletics, there is good news and not-so-good news, according to the study, "Women in Intercollegiate Sport." In 2014, 22.3 percent of athletic directors were women, an increase of about 20 percent since 2012, and employment of women in all areas of intercollegiate sports, including coaching, reached an all-time high in 2014. But that year, just over 11 percent of schools had no women in any administrative jobs. The study found that Division III schools were more likely to not have women in administrative jobs but were more likely to have women ADs. Other statistics from 2014 include:

- Of the 1,185 new administrative jobs created since 2004, 23 percent went to women
- 19.5 percent of Division I schools had female head athletic trainers; the number was higher at Division II and III schools
- Schools in the Northeast are more likely to have women as their head athletic trainer
- 7.7 percent of Division I schools had a female SID

level athletic directors. At a Division I school with a successful football program, an AD could earn more than $1 million per year. The range can go down to the low six figures, and salaries are even lower at Division II and III schools. Positions below the AD pay less. A school's size, division, location, and emphasis on the importance of successful athletic teams all influence the kind of salaries paid.

A 2013 report from the *St. Louis Post-Dispatch* looked at the salaries for the University of Missouri athletics department. Some sample salaries were:

Athletic director's office	$61,100 to $301,916
Athletic maintenance	$57,222
Communications	$30,500 to $75,000
Compliance	$40,000 to $85,000
Ticket office	$70,000

Figures like these are available for most public colleges and universities, while private schools do not have to disclose it. Workers at public schools receive **benefits** that match what other state employees get, and these vary from one state to the next. Benefits at private schools vary depending on the size of the school and its budget. Again, a Division III school typically cannot match what a large Division I school can offer.

It's not all watching sports: Any athletic department job will include lots and lots of paperwork

Finding Time and Privacy

Across the board, people who work in college athletics stress that one of the hardest parts of their job is the time required of them. People looking for a 9-to-5 job and weekends off will not find that in most positions. Games are often played on nights and weekends, and people in the ticket office, coordinators of

Working as a college sports athletic trainer means long hours. Starting with office work in the mornings, a work day might include a long trip and a whole evening in the arena, too.

student workers, communication staffers, and others have to be at those events. And those hours are on top of the regular Monday through Friday workdays.

Certain positions, such as sports information director and athletic trainer, also require traveling to away games. Those trips are strictly business, leaving little time for sightseeing, and can mean getting back home in the early morning. Some universities do offer "comp" time for such trips. That means that hours spent on the road can be made up with days off, usually over the summer, when demand for college sports work is greatly reduced while students are on summer break.

All those demands, said Tyler Geivett, mean that "there is a big struggle to have a family or life outside the job." In communications in particular, he said, there is a lot of **burnout** and job turnover. The stress of being SID led Kyle Muncy to leave that position and take another at UConn with more normal business hours. At times, he had to celebrate family birthdays in hotel rooms when the basketball team was traveling.

People in the athletic director's office have other pressures. At some public universities, Michael Cross wrote, "many states have '**sunshine laws**' that make virtually anything you write or do related to your job public information." At some private schools, ADs might face almost the same public scrutiny, since so many people focus on the business of college athletics and the success or failure of certain teams. Cross wrote, "There is little if anything about your life, your job, and your decision making that will be confidential as an athletic director."

A veteran athletic director like Mark Massari understands that his job might be enjoyable, but it comes with many responsibilities.

Challenges On and Off the Field

Day to day, ADs and their staff have other concerns. The athletic director hires people, but also has to fire them, which is never easy. More than most positions in college sports, the athletic director acts like an executive at a large company. His or her office has to take care of all of its employees, while also directing their work. That can mean as much time spent on administration as on athletics.

College sports departments also face financial hurdles. At times, a lack of money might mean dropping a sport, which disappoints the students playing it, the coaches, and the fans. Athletic directors also have to face the media and fans after a tough loss or a losing season. In 2014, the University of Alabama–Birmingham got national headlines when it decided to drop its football program.

"You have to be able to speak realistically but also in a positive fashion about the future of a program and where you hope it will go," noted LMU AD William Husak on the subject of having to cut teams.

Off the field, following all the NCAA rules is a challenge for entire athletic departments. Husak said, "You spend so much time documenting that you're **compliant** that it's hard to get work done."

An athlete's actions outside of school can cause problems, too. Oregon State's Mark Massari said, "You've got 500 kids, and 498 do the right thing, and two don't, and that's what makes the press."

When an athlete breaks the law or otherwise makes a bad decision, various members of the athletic department have to work to repair the school's image.

People in college athletics know that most student athletes are between the ages of 18 and 22. They're young, and some can be immature. Kyle Muncy found that one of the challenges of his job was tracking down athletes for interviews and other commitments he had arranged. "They're sitting down in the locker room knowing that you're going to come chasing them," he said. "There's a lot of time and effort expended doing that."

Reaching one of the NCAA's 39 national championship events, such as the College World Series, is a year-long struggle at every level of a college athletic department.

Coaches working at colleges have to fight constant battles in recruiting student-athletes for their programs. They face annual tests of their knowledge of the rules of that process.

"We are required to take a test once a year in order to be allowed to recruit off-campus," said Tim Vom Steeg, the men's soccer coach at UCSB who led them to the 2006 NCAA title. "We also get together as a staff to review some of the old rules and look into new or proposed rules. It is a steady drumbeat in terms of staying on top of the changes. For the past 15 or 16 years, you could have taken the test and waited five years and taken it again with no problem. But these days, the changes come literally with each single cycle. It's fast-moving."

For many who work in college athletics, however, all the hard work on and off the field is worth it as they watch their students begin to mature and have success on and off the field.

Text-Dependent Questions

1. What is one main reason that college athletics staffers find it hard to maintain a personal life?

2. Of the new jobs created in college sports since 2004, what percent went to women? Was it over or under 25 percent?

3. What substance did college sports expert Al Ferrer use to describe the starting salaries in many college positions?

Research Project

Look for a recent college athletics scandal. Read up on it and pay close attention to how the school responded. Count the number of people who spoke for the school and note their titles. How did what they said try to ease the situation in the school's favor?

Words To Understand

eligibility: a student's ability to compete in sports, based on grades or other school or NCAA requirements

logos: distinct pictures or words that represent a sports team, especially its nickname

liaison: a person who connects to groups to help them share information

spreadsheets: computer programs that calculate numbers and organize information in rows and columns

The Nitty-Gritty

When he's not at a game or in his office, William Husak (in red at left) sets aside time each day to walk. But it's not for exercise; Husak strolls across the campus at Loyola Marymount to visit with his coaches.

Husak might hear that a student athlete is not studying as much as he should, or that a coach is clashing with someone else in the athletic department. When there is an issue between employees, Husak talks to each one to get his or her side of the story. "You try to resolve an issue in the early stages before it becomes major"—an approach he takes with all the problems he hears about.

CHAPTER 4

Connecting with People

ADs and their staff rely on their talents of getting along with people and solving problems to keep their departments running smoothly. Communicating well with people and listening to them are key parts of the job.

Jim Philips made that kind of personal attention to his staff a priority when he became AD at Northwestern University in Evanston, Illinois (he later became vice president of athletics and recreation). He told *Forbes* magazine, "When I first got to Northwestern, within the first three months I had individual meetings with every single one of the more than 170 staff members in the department at the time, even our janitors and groundskeepers. I asked each of them to create…a one-page sheet telling me anything and everything they wanted me to know about them. I definitely received some funny looks, but it also made them realize that I cared about what they thought from day one."

ADs have to build the same kind of trust with athletic recruits. When Husak meets with recruits and their parents, he asks them what they are looking for in a college experience. Loyola Marymount wants good athletes and good students, and he wants recruits to feel sure that his school is right for them. Some athletic departments put less emphasis on the academic side of the college experience.

Underneath the AD, his deputy, associate, and assistant directors have the same responsibility to connect with others

The business of selling tickets falls to the athletic department and is a key source of revenue.

as part of their daily routine. But they also have to immerse themselves in the details of their particular tasks. At Oregon State, deputy AD Mark Massari focuses more on the external side of the department, looking at such things as marketing and ticket sales. In a day's worth of meetings, one might include discussing possibly changing the image on the football team's helmets.

That might seem like a small detail, but it could have a marketing impact. Massari said, "We make replica helmets, [but] will the fans enjoy the change, is there a recruiting angle to having unique helmets?" College sports teams strive for colorful **logos**, which can attract fans to buy clothing and other items featuring the logo, providing another source of revenue.

Every part of marketing is important, as it helps bring in money for the program. While Oregon State is not a small school, it's not a football powerhouse like its Pac-12 Conference rival, the University of Southern California (USC). With its much larger stadium and grander football tradition, USC can earn $4 million in ticket sales from just one game—almost three times what Oregon State can take in from a home game. People involved with generating revenue for an athletic department approach their jobs as other business executives do. Massari said, "We see a lot of **spreadsheets**, a lot of [revenue] projections." Massari and others have to watch revenues and expenses closely so they at least match or even to have more revenues than costs.

Getting Out the Message

In a different part of the external side of college athletics, staff in the communications department spend much of their time

A Blending of Two Worlds

Running a specific sports team requires staff workers who spend most of their time handling details away from the field. But at times, these people work with athletes, too. The people who have a foot in both administration and sports activities are called directors of operations. In 2010, Jan Bethea was named director of basketball operations (DOBO) for the University of Nebraska's women's team. Speaking later to IOU Sports, she described some of her duties: "As a DOBO you wear a lot of hats. I am primarily responsible for overall administrative side of the program . . . First and foremost, I am in charge of making sure we stay within our operating budget—and each year that gets harder. I am the liaison for the following departments: marketing, academic, development, housing, ticket office, facilities, sports information, business office, alumni, booster club, and many more. I also supervise our student managers and graduate assistant and serve as the office manager of our department.

"My day-to-day responsibility is to handle all speaking engagements for my head coach, speak with our team's academic advisor to check on grade progress, handle all scheduling needs for visiting teams, schedule our games for the upcoming season, monitor our incoming freshmen to make sure they have submitted in all their paperwork for admission and NCAA eligibility requirements . . ." Bethea summed up her role this way: "My job is to make sure the only thing the coaches have to think about is coaching."

Directors of operations also help coaches by showing players videos of games or helping them learn a team's playbook. But they can't actively take part in practices. They do play a part in recruiting, too, but only on their school's campus.

working with the media. The staff's goal is to give reporters accurate information whenever they need it. Writing up this information or creating stories for the school's Web site is an important part of Tyler Geivett's job. He tells students interested in a sports communications job, "If writing's not their thing, I would probably push them away from this line of work."

One specific piece of writing that comes out of the sports information office is the script for the public address (PA) announcer to follow during the game. As fans, people probably

don't think much about what the announcer is saying during a game. But along with introducing players or reporting on some of the events on the court or field, PA announcers also read information provided by the communications staff.

The public address announcer at most games works from a script prepared by the sports information staff.

To prepare to write the script, the staff member meets with people from the marketing and corporate relations departments. When Geivett prepares a script, he said, "I have to make sure that all of our contracts with corporate sponsors [are followed]." Each sponsor is mentioned several times during a sporting event. The script also lays out the order of activities that are common to sporting events—when the national anthem is sung, when starting lineup should be introduced, etc. Announcers also read conference news or information about upcoming games for a school's different teams.

Many college sporting events also have games that fans can participate in during timeouts or other breaks in the action. The information about these games and who is sponsoring them also goes into the PA script. The kind of game or contest is sometimes based on the crowd expected. If the marketing department recruited a lot of kids' groups or teams to a particular game, the games are oriented toward children. Other ticket sale promotions might have targeted students at the school, so the games will be geared toward them. The various external departments have to work together to help communications people deliver the script appropriate for each game. The goal, Geivett said, is to create a positive game day atmosphere for the fans.

Keeping reporters happy is also an important part of a SID's job. The media, whether print, broadcast, or online, help publicize a school's teams and keep fans informed. To help the reporters do their jobs, communications staffers prepare game notes before every event.

Before writing the notes, the staff member has to do research on the players, look for information about past meetings with the opponent, and maybe include a "this day in history" fun fact. Much of this information comes from the media guides that the communications departments assemble before the start of the season. The game notes also include current individual and team stats. This part of the job requires research skills, and it's one reason Kyle Muncy said that "a journalism background is very, very helpful" when starting down the path of working in sports communications.

Taking the Long View

While a communications staff deals with the day-after-day needs of providing information, some departments use a much longer time frame when looking at an athletic department's needs. For Jon Spaventa, renovating a 60-year-old gym on the UCSB campus meant first getting the money, thanks to a

Keeping college arenas like UCSB's Thunderdome up and running is a group effort made by many parts of the university's athletic department.

student vote, and then working with people from both on and off campus during the project, which spanned several months. Spaventa met with the construction firm, an architect, a project manager, and a student body that provided input on the project's direction. Speaking of the students, Spaventa said, "We report back to them on progress and let them know how the money is being spent." Even details like the color and location of signs inside the building are reviewed, trying to take into account the different tastes of the people involved. While the outside contractor did the actual work, Spaventa and his staff monitored their progress and at the end, checked to make sure everything was done correctly.

The College Athletics Experience

A love of sports is what draws people like Jon Spaventa to a career in college athletics. This book has only touched on some of the many options available. No matter what a person's personality, he or she can find a job, provided they take the right classes and are willing to take the initiative. "You can acquire the knowledge and the experience," Spaventa said. "But you have to have the desire and the work ethic."

Some of that knowledge can be gained outside the classroom. Mark Massari recommends students arrange interviews with people who do what they aspire to do. And that means doing some research before going in to understand the basics of the department and specific position, so the student can ask intelligent questions.

Once landing a job, the new hires in college athletics need to do any job they're asked to do. For Massari early in his career, that meant having his boss's coffee poured every morning. But from that simple start, he worked his way up to his position at Oregon State. That experience highlights one of Kyle Muncy's beliefs: "You can't ever think you're too big for any particular job…any and all experience is good."

With new experience, flexibility, and a desire to work hard, a person can succeed in a career in college athletics, which presents many rewards. Many would agree with Muncy's satisfaction with his job: "I get paid to be involved with sports… It's hard to complain too much about that."

Text-Dependent Questions

1. What are some of the responsibilities of a director of basketball operations?

2. What are some of the things a SID needs to include in a PA script?

3. Which school makes more from a football game in ticket sales, USC or Oregon State?

Research Project

Look at some college sports logos. Can you find a school whose logo has changed several times over the years? Why do you think they made those changes? See if you can find out if sales of their merchandise rose after the changes were made.

Find Out More

Books

Billings, Andrew C., Michael L. Butterworth, and Paul D. Turman. *Communication and Sport: Surveying the Field.* Los Angeles: SAGE Publications, 2015.

Freedman, Jeri. *Dream Jobs in Sports Management and Administration.* New York: Rosen Publishing, 2013.

Greenwell, T. Christopher, Leigh Ann Danzey-Bussell, and David J. Shonk. *Managing Sport Events.* Champaign, Ill.: Human Kinetics, 2014.

Web Sites

College Sports Information Directors of America
www.cosida.com/

North American Society for Sports Management
www.nassm.com/

Sports Business school programs
www.allbusinessschools.com/business-careers/sports-management/job-description/

Women in Sports Media
awsmonline.org/

Series Glossary of Key Terms

academic: relating to classes and studies

alumni: people who graduate from a particular college

boilerplate: a standard set of text and information that an organization puts at the end of every press release

compliance: the action of following rules

conferences: groups of schools in which schools within a group play each other frequently in sports

constituencies: a specific group of people related by their connection to an organization or demographic group

credential: a document that gives the holder permission to take part in an event in a way not open to the public

eligibility: a student's ability to compete in sports, based on grades or other school or NCAA requirements

entrepreneurs: people who start their own companies

freelance: a person who does not work full-time for a company, but is paid for each piece of work

gamer: in sports journalism, a write-up of a game

intercollegiate: something that takes places between two schools, such as a sporting event

internships: positions that rarely offer pay but provide on-the-job experience

orthopedics: the branch of medicine that specializes in preventing and correcting problems with bones and muscles

objective: material written based solely on the facts of a situation

recruiting: the process of finding the best athletes to play for a team

revenue: money earned from a business or event

spreadsheets: computer programs that calculate numbers and organize information in rows and columns

subjective: material written from a particular point of view, choosing facts to suit the opinion

Index

Credits

About the Author

Michael Burgan has written more than 250 books for children and teens, as well as newspaper articles and blog posts. Although not an athlete, he has written on both amateur and professional sports, including books on the Basketball Hall of Fame, the Olympics, and great moments in baseball. He lives in Santa Fe, New Mexico, with his cat Callie.

5